Guarded by God

Guarded by God

SHAMARA SCHAUF

iUniverse, Inc.
Bloomington

GUARDED BY GOD

iUniverse books may be ordered through booksellers or by contacting:

iUniverse
1663 Liberty Drive
Bloomington, IN 47403
www.iuniverse.com
1-800-Authors (1-800-288-4677)

ISBN: 978-1-4620-4682-9 (sc)
ISBN: 978-1-4620-4683-6 (ebk)

Printed in the United States of America

iUniverse rev. date: 09/14/2011

GUARDED BY GOD

How I Survived Anorexia and living with my Mood disorder

By Shamara Schauf-Dorgan

I do not know exactly when my eating disorder began, but it was, I believe, at a very young age. Perhaps I was born predisposed to it. I do know, however, that I have struggled with eating (or rather *not* eating) for practically my whole life. I have also suffered terribly from a severe mood disorder. During certain periods of my life, I have felt very high and energized; during other times, I have felt so low and depressed that I would lock myself in my bedroom, bawl my eyes out and wish to die. Eventually, I developed *anorexia nervosa*; it was a way for me get control of my life, both mentally and physically. I felt better when

I was in control. Although I have always been a picky eater, my eating disorder became worse when I felt most depressed or when there was a situation in which I felt emotionally threatened. There have been three times in my life when my weight has dropped to eighty pounds. In the last period of my anorexia, I even dropped to seventy pounds before I was hospitalized. During the in-between stages, I somehow managed to eat better and get my weight back up to a healthy level.

My name is Shamara. I was born on January, 19 1980 and, even though I was a full-term baby, I weighed only four pounds, seven ounces,. The doctors told my mother that her placenta was the size of a golf ball and that I had not been getting enough nutrition from her placenta during the last month of her pregnancy. In addition, my mother had complications during her delivery: she lost oxygen, couldn't breathe, and was given oxygen to help her through. At this time, she also had an out-of-body experience. She did not tell me about this until later in life. She said that she felt that she was floating in the air, as if her soul had left her body. She saw herself below, lying on the bed, about to give birth to me. Then she felt herself floating down a long, dimly glowing tunnel with a big bright light at the end. In the middle of the light, she saw a figure with extended arms welcoming her as she floated down the tunnel. She said that this gave her the most beautiful feeling in the world. She spoke to the figure and said, "God, if that is you, I am not ready to go yet. Please let me give birth to my child and let me enjoy her." Instantly, like the snapping of fingers, she was back in her body, and two minutes later I was born.

When she came to naming me, my mother considered two possible names: Shameriah, a Hebrew name, and Sabrina. She ended up combining the two as Shamara because Shameriah was too long and she loved the *a* ending of Sabrina. She gave my name the meaning, "Guarded by God" because, although I was a full-term baby, I was very small, but, based on her out-of-body experience, under divine protection. Subsequently, my name also came to

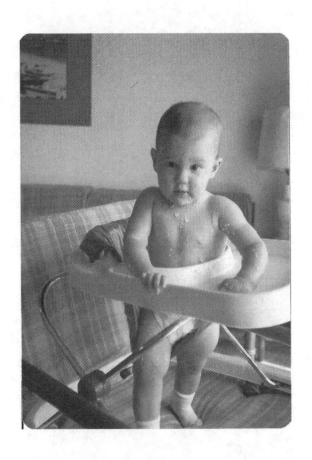

be connected to my overcoming my eating and mood disorders.

As I mentioned before, I cannot pinpoint the exact age that I was when my eating disorder started. However, I remember an incident when I was eight years old and in the second grade. The young boys in my class would continually tease me, saying terrible, terrible things like, "You are the ugliest girl in the world!" For a long time, I would stand up for myself and bluntly say back to them, "You don't know all the girls in the world, so how do you know that I am the ugliest?" However, little did I realize that the more that they were teasing me, the more I was internalizing my hurt feelings. I began to feel worthless, hopeless, depressed and not good enough to please anybody. I started to believe that I really was the ugliest girl in the world. I also remember feeling that I was in my own little world, consumed by sad thoughts which slowly became obsessive over time.

One day my father came to school with me to talk to my teacher and fellow classmates about this issue. The class sat in a circle on the classroom floor with me and my father in the middle. He told the students that I was very hurt and upset by the name-calling and he implored the students to stop. Although the name-calling gradually ended, I never forgot this experience, which left me emotionally tormented. From then on, I don't remember ever feeling truly happy with myself. I have always felt as if I've been wearing a mask all my life. I could never fully engage in activities like other children without feeling as if I was forcing myself to. I was always holding myself back because I felt continuously depressed. I never felt good enough or pretty enough to succeed in anything that I did. So I secluded myself in my negative thoughts, looking every day for a way out. Eventually, I wanted somebody to notice, somebody to care about me, but I did not know how to explain the way I was feeling. It was then that I experienced my first of three episodes of severe anorexia.

When I was twelve years old, my mother entered me in a fashion show at a local plaza. Although I was very excited to be in the show, I really didn't

feel pretty or perfect enough to be a model since I was already super thin. I was just starting to go through puberty and I hated my body. Before the show, I remember looking in the mirror at the clothes that I was wearing and thinking I looked fat. At meal times, I was already refusing to eat. It wasn't that I didn't like eating, or didn't want to eat. My poor eating habits were caused by feelings of depression. I felt continuously numb with no desire for food. I had a secret problem, one which was not only emotional, but physical too. My parents were unaware of this since I kept it to myself, even though at times I just wanted to escape. This is when I decided that the only way I could feel good about myself was by controlling the amount of food that I consumed. My illness became worse two years later when I entered high school.

I was fourteen now and absolutely loved exercising! Exercising for hours was my passion. I would do jumping jacks all the time, no matter what mood that I was in, happy, sad, or angry. I would wake up at four or five every morning and do at least a thousand quick jumping jacks before going to school. If I didn't do at least a thousand or if I was interrupted, I would stop and start all over again. Sometimes repeating them made me late for school. The obsession with exercise started to take over my life.

At school during lunch hour I would be starving because my early morning workout had left me no time for breakfast. I would feel so anxious about this that I would hurry to the cafeteria to buy and eat all the food that I could get. Once there, however, I ignored my hunger pangs and just buy one small muffin for lunch. I would carefully rip off its edges to make it even smaller and eat only the core. When finished, I would quietly excuse myself from the table and go do jumping jacks in the washroom. During my four years in high school, I followed the same eating ritual every day. After school, I never took part in any extracurricular activities or spent much time hanging out with friends; instead I would rush home as fast as I could to do another thousand jumping jacks. My eating decreased even more and the weight scale became my new best friend.

At bedtime, before I could relax and fall asleep, I had to do another thousand jumping jacks.

By December of 1997, my weight was down to eighty pounds. During the Christmas holidays, I managed to start eating better and gained back ten pounds in two weeks. After the holidays, my schoolmates told me that they could see a difference in how I looked. I had only gained ten pounds, but for someone as thin as I was, the change was really noticeable. I felt proud of myself too. I also drank a lot of a meal-replacement drink called *Ensure*. Although I continued to do my jumping jacks, I had gained much of my weight back several months later. I now weighed 110 pounds, about ten to twenty pounds under my optimum weight.

My worst episode of anorexia struck at age twenty-one, when I dropped to a potentially fatal seventy pounds. I had just broken up with my boyfriend of two years, someone whom I had been pretty certain I was going to marry. But he turned out to be verbally abusive. The only way that I could escape the effects of this

and feel better about myself was, once again, by controlling the amount of food I ate. Hoping that I could change him and be happy again, I hung on to this relationship as long as I could. But I was unsuccessful. And I was dying in the process. After all, how could *he* make me happy, if I was not even happy with myself? Everything in my life seemed to be going wrong and falling out of place.

I had a part-time job, working every Thursday, Friday and Saturday evenings as a customer-service rep and cashier for the LCBO. At the time, I enjoyed working there, even though it was obvious to customers that I was anorexic. I may have looked like a walking skeleton, but this didn't bother me since I didn't think there was anything wrong with my appearance. In spite of my frail condition, I managed to go to work and to do my job every shift. It wasn't long, however, before the store manager took me aside and told me that I would have to take some time off work and get well. I was no longer being allowed to work because I had become both a concern and a risk both to myself and to my fellow employees.

Because I was so thin and frail, they were afraid that I might have a work-related accident. Fortunately, I didn't. But I didn't like having to take sick leave one bit because going to work was an escape for me as it allowed me, if only for a few hours, to get my mind off myself. This also meant that sooner or later I would have to face reality and overcome my illness, if I wanted to get better.

So, I was sent home. As soon as I arrived, I did the first thing that I always did when I felt angry. And this particular time I felt extremely angry. I went down to the basement and began doing jumping jacks like a woman possessed. I didn't want to stop. As I exercised, I began to wonder: Would being off work make life worse for me—or better.? This was a determination that I felt I had to make and one that I could no longer run away from. My parents were now worrying about me constantly. They both felt totally helpless in the situation, even though, they were completely supportive of me. So this time while I was doing my jumping jacks in the basement, my parents called 911. My mother

explained the situation to the operator and an ambulance arrived at my house minutes later to take me to emergency. I argued that this was a waste of time. But my parents were so worried and insistent that finally I agreed to go, if only to give them peace of mind. Once I arrived to the hospital I had to wait like everybody else did in emergency. I believed that once a doctor saw me, that I would just be sent home because I did not have an injury and my illness was not life-threatening. In fact, the emergency doctor did send me home, explaining that my family therapist and doctor could help me because I was officially in their care.

Not only were my parents supportive of me, so were my two sisters. The family helped me in different ways. My father believed that, if he could understand me and my illness, then he could help me, but only if I chose to help myself too. He actually did help me a lot. For one, he would check on me in bed in the middle of the night to make sure I was still breathing. For another, he researched information about anorexia on the internet. He desperately hoped that he might find

time as it needed. Even though, deep down, I was afraid of trying to overcome my anorexia, my desire to get better was now stronger than my fear. I had had enough of my old self, I had suffered far too long and I had caused others to suffer as well. It helped too that I was now away from the place where my anorexia rituals—the over-exercising, the under-eating (now down to a spoonful of yoghurt and granola) and the obsessive-thinking—were chiefly performed. Yes, I was now away from home.

By the time I arrived at the hospital, it was 5:00pm, and already dinner time in the eating disorder unit. The nurse handed me a tray of food that contained larger portions than a normal person would eat. The size of the meals was based on your particular body weight; in order to gain weight, you had to eat larger and larger portions so that you would thereby overcome your fear of counting calories. With each meal, the calories were increased. Eventually, you even had to eat a dessert, which usually was a slice of pie, or a piece of chocolate fudge cake. For my first meal, the nurses gave me two large honey-glazed chicken breasts with a mound of gravy on top of the chicken, rice and steamed carrots. Butter was then to be put on the vegetables. We were not allowed to drink any liquids during meal times because liquids filled you up. I remember how appetizing the meal looked. Now if I could only get myself to eat it! A half hour before each meal, all the patients were given a special pill designed to inflate your stomach so you could fit lots of food in your stomach without feeling full. Our stomachs and organs had all shrunk due to our not eating for so long.

I shocked the doctors and nurses because I ate my entire meal faster than the forty-five minutes we were given to do so. A normal person will typically consume a meal in this time, and our goal was to learn to eat like a normal person or what the doctors called "people without eating disorders". All of us in the clinic (there were only woman at this time) had to eat all the food that we were given on our plates. We were put to be on a fixed meal schedule to get us used to eating three meals a day, just like a normal person would eat. Breakfast was at 8:00 am, lunch at 12:00 pm and dinner at 5:00 pm, with snack times in between. I was very proud that I had eaten all my dinner without a problem. I was able to do this, I believe, because I was now motivated and away from home. But I had one question for the doctors that I could never answer myself. I wondered why, no matter what weight I had been during my life, I always suffered with depression, mood swings and disturbing thoughts? So I asked one of the doctors. I tried explaining to him that, in addition to anorexia, I was also suffering from a mood disorder. Could the two disorders be connected, I asked. But he wouldn't take me seriously. He dismissed my question outright, explaining that when I gained my weight back, the mood disorder would disappear too, since it was only weight-related. I couldn't believe it! After all, the main reason that I had refused to eat as a child was because I felt feelings of depression. And even as I write this, although I am presently back to a healthy weight, I continue to suffer from depression and mood swings. When I think back, I could have had this doctor in serious trouble for not taking my concern seriously.

I was in the Inpatient program for Eating Disorders for four weeks. It was a very healing time, yet an emotional one too. I learned new eating strategies, and gained all my weight back. Most importantly, it saved my life. Still, the experience brings back a few unhappy memories that are seen in all areas of my life. I believe that for every negative experience, there is always something positive to be learned from it. I shared my room with another woman who was also anorexic. The unit was divided into two bedrooms by a white curtain. Each unit was decorated differently since we were permitted to decorate our rooms the same way we decorated our bedrooms at home in order to make us feel more comfortable. There was a bathroom in the rooms for anorexic patients, but not in the rooms for bulimic patients because of their need to purge themselves: they had to use an external bathroom and only in the company of a nurse. Although the doctors and nurses were friendly, the floor rules were strict. For example, women who used exercise as a purging technique were not allowed to do any exercising. Before entering the program, I had always exercised after I ate; now that was out of the question. We were not even allowed to talk on the telephone while standing up. Instead, we had to be seated since any form of motion would be considered burning calories and we needed all the calories we could get in order to gain weight and to become healthy again.

Just before I was admitted to hospital, I went out for a run one morning—after finishing my jumping jacks routine, of course. Every day, I would run by a young woman pushing an elderly lady in a wheelchair. This time for some reason, I decided to stop and introduce myself to them. It turned out, however, that the young attendant could not speak English. Although shy and timid, she seemed very kind and friendly. I felt a warm and calming saintly energy coming from her as soon as we met. I wanted to explore this feeling and get to know her better in spite of the language barrier. So we started communicating with hand gestures and vocal sounds. From her expression, I could tell that she liked me too and that we had an immediate connection. I walked home with her as she pushed the elderly

woman in the wheel chair. Outside her house I met another woman named Anne who spoke English. I asked Anne what the young woman's name was. She told me her name was Ludmyla and that she came from the Ukraine. She was the same age as me, twenty-one. Ludmyla, a devout Catholic, had come to Canada on a visa arranged by the Church. Ludmyla accepted my offer to teach her English and take her on a tour of Toronto. Ludmyla had a very strong faith in God and was thinking about entering a convent. From the on, we became the best of friends and still are to this day. She was also a bride's maid in my wedding and is the god mother of my first born son, David. Even though I was anorexic when I met Ludmyla, my disorder didn't interfere with my ability to care for others and to want to help those in need of assistance. Helping others feel good about themselves, has helped me feel better about myself. One evening when Ludmyla was visiting me at the hospital, I asked the nurse to arrange a surprise party for her since it was Ludmyla's birthday. As he brought in a birthday cake and sang Happy Birthday to her, I felt so happy that I could do this for new friend. So we

all ate birthday cake in the hospital and celebrated Ludmlya's twenty-second birthday. This was one of my happiest memories from my time in hospital. But here's an even happier memory: A month after being admitted, I was able to leave the hospital. I had gained thirty pounds and now weighed one hundred pounds, the minimum weight for leaving the hospital. Thirty pounds certainly sounds like a lot of weight to gain in one month, but remember that I was on a fixed diet with plenty of calories, which were increased weekly. Back at home, I continued to eat the way I had learned in the hospital; three months later, I weighed 117 pounds.

In January, 2003, I turned twenty-four. I decided to celebrate my recovery and my new life with a big birthday party. Because I had by now gained back all my weight, my parents supported the idea. I was still getting used to my new body shape and size. Even now when I look at photos of myself from that time, I think my face looks fat. But I know that this is not the case, merely a symptom of my illness. More importantly, however, it was at this celebration that I met my

future husband. He was an unexpected guest, the friend of a schoolmate named Peter and his fiancé Lucy. Peter asked me if his brother John Paul and his friends could come to the party. I said, "Sure, the more people, the better!" I even phoned John Paul and gave him directions to my house. Earlier that week, my mother and I had had a discussion about marriage. I distinctly remember her saying, "Now wouldn't it be funny if God rewards you with the man of your dreams and you get married this year for reaching your goals, gaining weight and becoming healthy again." I thought that there was no way I would be getting married. I didn't even have a boyfriend and after what I had been through, I just wanted to take care of myself. As it turned out, half way through the party, my girl friend Sabina told me that John Paul wanted to take me out on a date. I told her to tell him that I was flattered, but I wasn't interested, for as I just explained, I want nothing to do with men for the moment. But as midnight approached, I decided that I could at least talk to John Paul and get to know him a little better. I invited some of guests to stay and the rest is history, as they say. I can't explain why, but I felt a strong connection to John Paul right from the start. When I first talked to him on the phone, there was a affectionate tone to his voice that I fell in love with right away. We were engaged two months later and married six months after that in October, 2004.

My mother-in-law, Mary, has always been a very spiritual woman with a strong faith in God. She believes that if you turn your life over to God, He will take care of you and everything in life will fall into place. She is the happiest woman I know. Mary and I have now become close friends. Little did I know that before I met John Paul and his family, Lucy, his brother Peter's fiancé, had approached Mary the year before and told her about someone called Shamara who was in hospital, suffering from anorexia and struggling for her life. She asked Mary if she would pray for Shamara's recovery. To this day, Mary prays one hour every morning for all her family and friends and for anybody you ask her to, even if she doesn't know them. She prays that God will bring guidance, health and love to their lives. Two months after John Paul and I were married,

we were all at a family gathering at my mother-in-law's house. Lucy and I were talking. She suddenly remembered that she had previously spoken to Mary and asked her to pray for me when I was in the hospital. I couldn't believe what I was hearing! Instantly, I approached Mary and told her, "I'm the Shamara that you were praying for last year to recover from anorexia, you know, the girl Lucy asked you to pray for!" We both totally freaked out in amazement and felt chills from head to toe. Mary believes to this day that it was partly because of her praying for me that I am now alive and healthy. She believes that I am a walking miracle and that God brought me not only to John Paul, but to his family too for a good reason. So, you see, it's no coincidence that my name, Shamara, means "Guarded by God"!

I now have a beautiful two-year old son named David. He was born on Remembrance Day, November 11, 2007. Remembrance Day is the day we remember all our loved ones who have passed away in war. To me it is also a day of peace, hope and love. It is the day to celebrate the birth and life of my son David, but also my

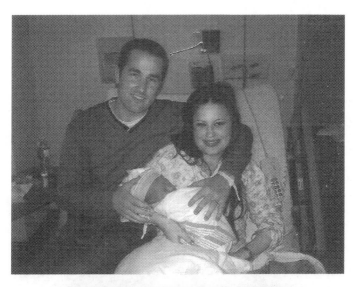

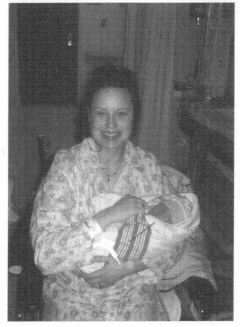

life as a new mother, one living without an eating disorder. I do not regret being anorexic; but I do not want to ever be that way again. I have learned and grown because of my painful experiences. I hope to continue to help myself move forward to a happier and healthier future and also to inspire others in their struggle with the disorder. As for my mood swings and depression, I am presently learning new ways to deal with these, and with God by my side, be the best person that I can be. After all, my name Shamara, does mean "Guarded by God"!

After all I've been through; the best advice that I can give anybody is still: "If God brought you to it, he will walk you through it". In life we all have choices. Unfortunately, we don't always make the right choices, and this can lead to negative consequences. But no matter how difficult the situation you find yourself in, you can always "walk" yourself through it if you really want to and believe you can. When you feel so low that you believe life can't get any worse and it can never improve, you are, I believe, in that particular situation for a reason and you can still make a positive choice. In my own case, I had to make the decision that I was important, special and deserved to be healthy—and then stick to it. No matter how much love and support I had from family and friends (and this did help very much), ultimately it was I alone who had to want to become healthy and no longer feel sorry for myself. Until I made that decision, I did not and could not improve. I also believe that it is often the strongest people that go through these experiences because God knows beforehand that they can get through them. In other words, certain people are meant to have these experiences in order to become walking examples and to teach others. Something positive can always be learned from every negative situation. You can accomplish anything you want in life if and when you put your heart into it. So remember: if God brought you to it, He will walk you through it safely. Believe in yourself. I do!

As I look back at my life exactly ten years later on June, 2011 I am coming to terms with myself and my anorexia, on new level of self-forgiveness. Before I was only doing the motions: the eating to gain my weight back because I was so severely underweight. I have carried around a deep burden for all those years. My goal for this upcoming year is moving forward to a much healthier, happier, positive, loving, joyful, wealthy, prosperous, new and exciting life, through the process of self -forgiveness, by living one day at a time with my family and friends.

I am so happy to have finally found my purpose. I am bringing joy, happiness, love and fulfillment into others lives through my writings and personal experiences. Thank you for all your support. You all hold a very special place in my heart, whether I have known you from many years ago or I have just connected with you along this journey, because no one understands better that both men and women are beautiful both inside and out In other words, If God brought you to it, he will walk you through it safely!

A special thanks to my parents, sisters, Jocelynn Dalton, Sabina Lackner, Lisa Petko, Sylvia Jardanny, Veegee Evangelist, Linda, Lydmila Levchuck, Paula Disstefano, Karen Hope Zhou,

John Paul Dorgan and Mary Dorgan for all her prayers. Thanks for all your love and support and for never, ever losing faith in me. It is because of your help and love that I want to share my story and to help others in the world.

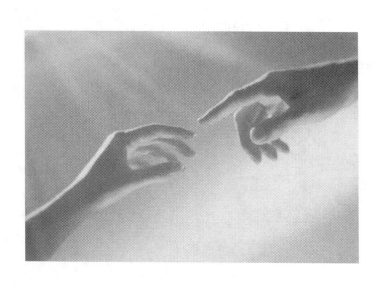

MISS JUMPING JACK

It was five pm, dinner time, when Gabriella entered the gloomy hospital dining room for the first time at the inpatient clinic for eating disorders. Twenty-one years old and weighing just seventy pounds, she was anxiously preparing herself for her first full meal in fifteen years. The clinic's doctors had given her, if she didn't succeed in their forced-eating program, only a month to live. Her stomach and vital organs had shrunk to half their size. She rarely went to the toilet. She had become so frail and emaciated; she looked like a walking skeleton. Anorexic on and off since childhood, Gabriella had recently decided that life was too precious to lose like this. To get healthy, however, she knew she had to get away from home and its daily rituals: the self-starving, the over-exercising and the obsessive thinking. Gabriella had been my next-door neighbor and best friend since childhood. Although I'd known for a long time that she had a serious eating disorder, only recently had she finally admitted to me that she was severely ill and needed my help. Her confession caused us both to cry in relief. Because Gabriella had always been stubborn and single-minded, her decision seemed to offer more hope than one might expect under the circumstances. After all, I reasoned, if being stubborn and single-minded had gotten her into this situation, it might also get her out of it.

*   *   *

Gabriella's eating disorder started when she was only eight years old. She was a special girl with a gorgeous smile, long brown hair, beautiful big brown eyes and a sensitive personality—too sensitive as things turned out. Whether a child can be born with an eating disorder, I am unsure. But I am sure that her condition began when Gabriella was in second grade. On a beautiful late summer day, she and I were doing each other's hair in the schoolyard before the morning bell rang. A classmate named Thomas, along with some other boys, suddenly ran over to us and started yelling repeatedly at Gabriella, "You're the ugliest girl in the world! You're the ugliest girl in the world! You're the ugliest girl in the world!" Gabriella stood up for herself and yelled back at them "You don't know all the girls in the world, so how do you know that I am the ugliest?" I guess I should have defended her, but I felt helpless and didn't know what to do. The boys continued to taunt Gabriella like this every day for the next three months. The more they teased her, the less she fought back and the more she internalized her sadness.

One afternoon, Gabriella's father came to school to speak to her teacher about his daughter's abuse. The teacher told the class that Gabriella was very upset because of their teasing and name-calling and that it had to stop. Gradually, the mistreatment ended. But Gabriella never forgot this experience. She was emotionally tormented and had little confidence in herself, especially in her appearance which from now on she would always consider ugly. As she grew up, I could see she was constantly wearing a mask and was never honest with herself. Unlike other kids, she didn't participate in school activities, unless forced to do so. I often remember her saying that she felt depressed and unworthy of love. She was obsessed by negative thoughts and I sensed that she was looking for a way out. She wanted somebody to notice her sickness, but couldn't explain the way she was feeling to anyone at the time. Not even to me, her best friend.

It was when Gabriella was twelve that I noticed that her condition was worsening. Her mother had entered her in a fashion show at a local mall. Before the event, I noticed a miserable expression on her face while she tried on her outfits. I watched as she kept examining her body in the mirror from head to toe. I asked what was wrong, but she wouldn't answer. My feeling was that she didn't think that she was good enough to be a model. Afterwards, she told me that she thought she looked fat in all the outfits, even though I insisted she was slender and a great model.

Gabriella's illness got worse when she was fourteen and in grade nine. At home she began refusing to eat. Up till then her parents had been largely unaware of the seriousness of her problem. It seemed I was the only one who knew her dangerous secret, that she could feel good about herself only when she ate as little as possible and exercised excessively. Strenuous workouts, especially doing jumping-jacks, became her passion. She would wake up at five every morning and do a thousand fast jumping-jacks before school. She told me that she always had to do a minimum of a thousand and that, if they were ever interrupted, she would have to start all over again. This often made her late for school. Her obsession with doing jumping-jacks began to take over her life. Sometimes she would exercise non-stop for eight hours. Meanwhile she was always starving but unwilling to eat. Since she never ate breakfast, Gabriella was so weak by lunchtime, she would be ill. She would then to go to the cafeteria ravenously hungry and determined to eat all the food that she could get. Once there, however, she would buy only a small muffin. I often watched as she ripped its edges off to make it even smaller, and then just ate the inside part. This became her eating ritual every day for five years of high school. When finished her muffin, Gabriella would excuse herself to the washroom and do a series of jumping-jacks to work it off. One day, a girl called Cassandra, considered the most popular female student in the school, walked into girls room while Gabriella was doing her exercise routine. Laughing hilariously at the strange sight,

Cassandra cruelly yelled at her, "Well, if it isn't Miss Jumping-Jack! No wonder you're so damn thin and ugly, freak!".

From then on, Gabriella was known in school as "Miss Jumping Jack". After classes, she spent less and less time with her friends because she wanted to go home and do a thousand jumping-jacks. At the same time, she hardly ate, merely picking at her meals and excusing herself from the table so she could go to her room and do more jumping-jacks. The weight scale now became her new best friend as she obsessed over her body image. She was frequently depressed. This set up a dangerous vicious cycle: the more depressed she became, the less she ate; the less she ate, the more depressed. Her weight, already low, now began to drop dangerously. At times, she would lock herself in her room, bawl her eyes out and wish herself dead. To relieve the sadness and help herself fall asleep at night, Gabriella would do a thousand jumping-jacks before going to bed. Every year when we celebrated our birthdays together, it was only with each other and in our bedrooms, since she felt anxious around large groups of people.

We'd never have a birthday cake because she was afraid to eat it. It didn't matter how much I tried to console her, nothing I said made sense to her when she felt down, which was now most of the time. I felt sorry for Gabriella, but all I could do was pray for her.

Things finally got so bad that her father began checking on her while she was asleep to see if she was breathing. Desperate to understand her condition, he searched the internet for information on her disease and wrote letters to the head doctors at the National Eating Disorder Clinic, seeking their advice. It was only when, by chance, Gabriella found these letters on his desk one day that she realized just how ill she had become and how much she was hurting her parents. It was the last straw. The next day, she finally agreed to join an inpatient program for eating disorders. A week later, she was squeezing my hand tightly as I lead her into the hospital.

*   *   *

As she sat down for her first meal at the clinic, a doctor gave Gabriella two pills, the first to inflate her stomach so she could eat comfortably without feeling the pressure of being full, and the second to act as a laxative. A nurse then handed Gabriella her tray of food. The portions were larger than a normal person would eat, with the exact size of the meal being based on the patient's weight. The patient had to eat enough food to reach her Body Mass Index (BMI) and overcome her fear of counting calories. With each meal, the number of calories was increased; eventually, the patient even had to eat dessert. For her first meal, Gabriella was given two large honey-glazed chicken breasts with rice and steamed carrots. She wasn't allowed to drink any liquids since these they would fill up her stomach. Since the goal was to teach the patients to eat normally, they had had to finish their meal within forty-five minutes. Unlike usual hospital fare, the food in the program looked and smelled delicious, and even made me feel hungry. But how would Gabriella react to this, her first full meal since age eight? I watched anxiously as she looked at her plate, took a deep breath, paused—and then suddenly picked up her fork and knife and began furiously eating. To my surprise, she consumed the entire meal in less than ten minutes. How could someone who is severely anorexic simply walk in, act as if there is nothing wrong, and bolt down every scrap of food on her plate? Looking up from her plate, Gabriella exclaimed to the shocked nurses and doctors, "I never knew hospital food tasted this great!." We all laughed in joy and relief.

The clinic's doctors and nurses were very sympathetic and supportive, but when it came to the rules, they enforced them with absolute strictness: any patient found disobeying these in the slightest way was sent home immediately. Like the other women in the program, Gabriella was put on a rigid eating schedule. The idea was to get her used to eating three meals a day. Breakfast was at 8:00 am, lunch at 12:00 pm and dinner at 5:00 pm sharp. There were also snacks served in-between. Since any form of motion would burn calories needed to gain weight and become healthy, all exercise was forbidden. And it was exercise, even more than not eating, that "Miss

Jumping Jack" now found hardest to quit. The rule was so strict that she wasn't even allowed to stand up while talking on the telephone. Through her remarkable determination, Gabriella made rapid progress. Within a month she tipped the scales at a hundred pounds, the weight required to leave the hospital and continue the program as an outpatient. In this second stage, she followed the same eating schedule as an inpatient, and took group therapy between meals. After just twelve weeks on this program, Gabriella weighed a healthy one hundred-and-thirty pounds. She glowed beautifully and looked twenty years younger. I was so proud and happy for her!

Three months later, to celebrate her birthday and her new life, Gabriella threw a party at her house. I came with Jim, my fiancé. At the last moment, we invited along his handsome, outgoing, life-of-the-party brother, John. All four of us had attended the same high school a few years before. Not long after we arrived, John pulled me aside and whispered excitedly, "Hey, the hostess is really beautiful! Can you introduce me to her?" Surprised that he hadn't recognized her, I didn't tell him who she was; I wanted it to be a surprise for both of them. But when I told Gabriella there was a handsome hunk who wanted to meet her, she said no thanks: after all she had gone through—the verbal abuse, the years of illness, the difficult recovery—men were the furthest thing from her mind. Towards the end of the party, however, she relented and decided she would meet her new admirer. "Wait a moment," John exclaimed as he was introduced to Gabriella. "Aren't you the girl at our high school they used to call Miss Jumping-Jack? I hardly recognized you. You used to be so thin . . ." "And ugly?" she replied. "No, no, you were never ugly," John said, firmly. "It was the way the kids at school picked on you that was ugly." From that evening on, Gabriella and John became inseparable. Two months later, they were engaged; six months later, married.

Nowadays, Gabriella is still my best friend, but also my sister-in-law. We spend a lot of time together raising our growing families. Because of what we've experienced together, we teach our children the following precepts: never hurt other kids with cruel language or nicknames; never keep bad feelings pent up inside you but tell others about them, and, most importantly, never ever underestimate the power of hope and love.